A CT'S MEMOIR

Copyright © 2023 Rebekah Troyer | All rights reserved

Copyright protects the voice of the author, encourages diversity of thought, creates space for uninhibited creativity, and adds value to the human experience. Thank you for buying this book and thereby promoting free speech. No portion of this book may be reproduced mechanically, electronically, or by any other means, including photocopy, without permission of the publisher or author except in the case of brief quotations embodied in critical articles and reviews. It is illegal to copy this book, post it to a website, or distribute by any other means without permission from the publisher or author.

The purpose of this book is to educate, inspire, and entertain as a work of creative nonfiction. The author and/or publisher shall have neither liability nor responsibility to anyone with respect to any loss or damage caused, or alleged to be caused, directly or indirectly by the information contained in this book.

PRINTED IN THE UNITED STATES OF AMERICA

WHERE THE HUMANS GO TO DIE

WRITTEN AND ILLUSTRATED BY REBEKAH TROYER

BEKS

THE MEG

LITTLE EM

BELLA

THE DOG

Hello Humans

My name is Bella, and I am a cat. I spent the first months of my life in a shelter, until my humans "rescued" me. Giving me what they would call "a loving home". I have three humans and, bless their little hearts, they attempt to care for me, but alas, it has become quite clear that they need my help more than I need theirs. I don't know what they would do without me, and if I don't care for them, who will?

There is Beks, the Meg, and little Em. Oh and I almost forgot about the dog which I don't even want to mention, but he is still a part of our family.

My life is full of many stories and happenings around my "In". So I have granted you a peek into a purrr-fect day in the life of a not-so-average house cat...

The first thing to know is that my humans don't seem to understand how time works.

Eventually, when the light disappears, they seem to just die. They lay motionless on a large soft thing called a "bed" and do nothing for hours!

Trust me, I am not exaggerating. I will never understand why they choose to sleep at night. Don't they know this is the best time to do all the things?

When my humans first brought me home, I slept right on my human's neck. Honestly, I was a little scared that she would just disappear.

But this didn't last too long. I soon discovered she wouldn't move, so I left my spot on her neck because I had much exploring to do.

At first, Beks kept the bedroom door shut, so I only had the room to explore, but there was much to find. There is the "underneath", under the place where my human sleeps.

It is a place of lost things.
For example, I find many of my human's clothes, shoes, and these little pieces of candy-scented paper.

Now in this room my human also has things I can climb on, like the large shelves she keeps her clothes in. She even leaves things on top of it.

Now at first I was too small to jump up and discover these things, but now I am big enough.

I think she leaves things there for me to push off. Because every time I get something to go on the floor, she picks it up and puts it back, and tells me "No!" I think that means she wants me to "do it again".

As her caretaker, I can't let Beks stay in the bed too long. She could die of starvation!! Even worse, I could die.

After I get my Beks to feed me, she tries to go back to her soft place, but that just doesn't work for me, because, of course, I need some attentions. What does she expect me to do? Socialize with the dog?

As the morning goes on, my humans layer themselves with many clothes and prepare for the places they must go in the "out". I don't understand why they must leave. Wouldn't it be better for them to stay in the "in" and spend time with me?

For the rest of the day it's just me, the Meg, and the dog. The Meg sits in a chair and pushes buttons on a light box all day. (A strange human habit, I suppose.) The good part is that she sits in a chair by the glass that looks into the "out".

I humor her, pretending that these imaginary tales are real. The dog thinks they are, and it makes little Em happy so I go along with it.

Scan me!

More Adventures with Bella

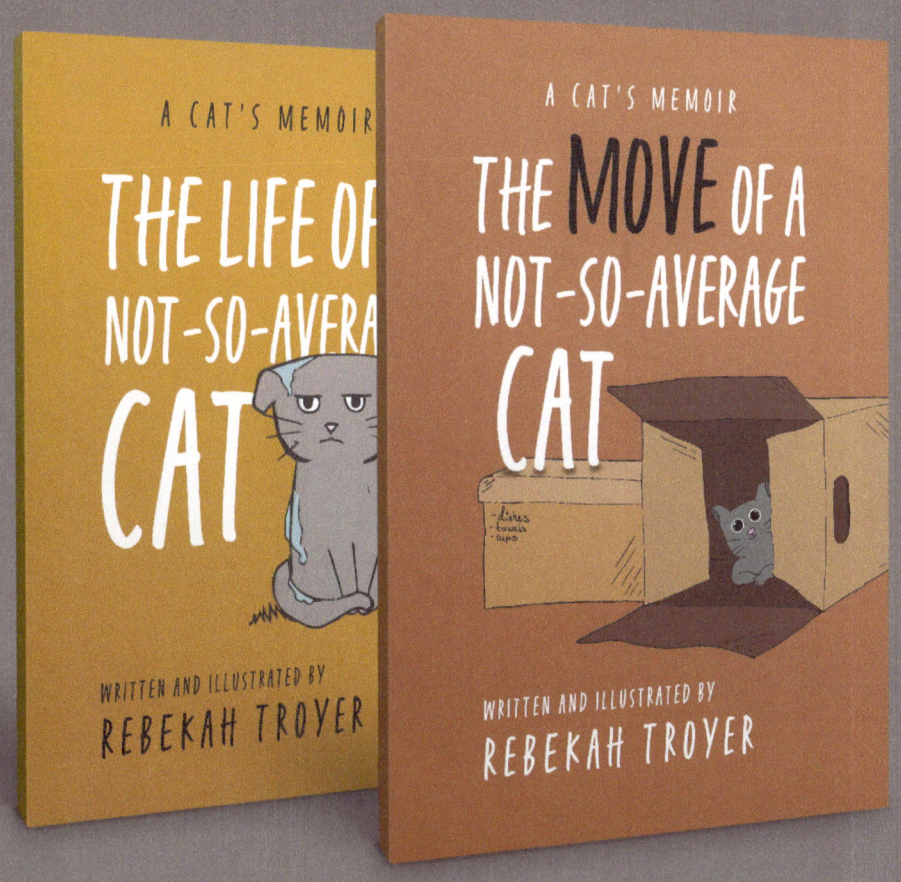

Don't keep Bella waiting! She's ready for the next adventure in her other books. Available on Amazon.

Meet the Author

Rebekah Troyer, often called Beks, is the renowned author behind "A Cat's Memoir" series that began during the Covid-19 lockdown with her first book "The Life of a Not-So-Average Cat". Growing up as the sixth of eight siblings, her love for cats and storytelling flourished early. Her unique bond with cats earned her the nickname 'Cat Whisperer'. Bella, the series' protagonist, was adopted in 2019 and inspired the stories Rebekah shared with her niece, Emma, which later evolved into the books in this series.

CONNECT WITH **Bekah**

 ACATSMEMOIR@GMAIL.COM

A CAT'S MEMOIR

www.ingramcontent.com/pod-product-compliance
Lightning Source LLC
Chambersburg PA
CBHW040726060526
44119CB00084B/339